Contents

Reptiles and amphibians

- **Reptiles** are scaly-skinned animals that live in many different habitats, mainly in warm regions. They include crocodiles, lizards, snakes and tortoises.

- **Reptiles are cold-blooded,** but this does not mean that their blood is cold. A reptile's body cannot keep its blood warm, and it has to control its temperature by moving between hot and cool places.

◄ *Like all reptiles, crocodiles rely on basking in the sunshine to gain energy for hunting. At night, or when it is cold, they usually sleep.*

•••● BULLETPOINTS ●•••

REPTILES &
AMPHIBIANS

John Farndon Ann Kay
Consultant: Steve Parker

Miles
Kelly
PUBLISHING

First published in 2005 by Miles Kelly Publishing Ltd
Bardfield Centre, Great Bardfield
Essex, CM7 4SL

Copyright © 2005 Miles Kelly Publishing Ltd
Some material in this book first appeared in *1000 Facts on Animals*

2 4 6 8 10 9 7 5 3 1

Editorial Director: Belinda Gallagher
Editorial Assistant: Hannah Todd **Designer:** Ian Paulyn
Picture Research: Liberty Newton **Production:** Estela Boulton

British Library Cataloguing-in-Publication Data
A catalogue record for this book is available from the British Library

ISBN 1-84236-578-9

Printed in China

www.mileskelly.net
info@mileskelly.net

ık the following artists who have contributed to this book:
tin Camm, Jim Channell, Richard Draper, Rob Jakeway,
es, Alan Male, Doreen McGuinness, Terry Riley,
Rob Sheffield, Sarah Smith, Steve Weston

ıres are from: Miles Kelly Archives; Corel

Newts are amphibians. The long, finlike crest on the back of this great crested newt becomes taller and more colourful in spring when the male attracts a female for mating. This large newt measures 17 cm.

● **Reptiles bask in the sunshine** to gain energy to hunt, and are often less active at cooler times of year.

● **A reptile's skin** looks slimy, but it is quite dry. It keeps in moisture so well that reptiles can survive in deserts. The skin often turns darker to absorb the Sun's heat.

● **Although reptiles grow** for most of their lives, their skin does not, so they must slough (shed) it every now and then.

● **Amphibians** are animals that live both on land and in water. They include frogs, toads, newts and salamanders.

● **Most reptiles** lay their eggs on land, but amphibians hatch out in water as tadpoles, from huge clutches of eggs called spawn.

● **Like fish**, tadpoles have gills to breathe in water, but they soon metamorphose (change), growing legs and lungs.

● **Amphibians** never stray far from water.

...FASCINATING FACT...
Reptiles were the first large creatures to live entirely on land, over 350 million years ago.

Biggest and smallest

- **Reptiles and amphibians** come in every size and shape. There are more than 6500 species of reptiles and 4000 species of amphibians.

- **The largest reptile** is the saltwater crocodile from the Indian and west Pacific Oceans. It measures a staggering 8 m from nose to tail.

- **The saltwater crocodile** has been known to attack humans and has been responsible for fatalities.

- **The Japanese giant salamander** is the largest amphibian in the world. It grows to around 1.5 m long and can live for over 50 years.

- **The Jaragua lizard** is the world's smallest reptile. Discovered in 2001, the lizard is native to the Caribbean and it measures just 16 mm from nose to tail.

- **The giant treefrog** is the largest frog in Australia. It is a tropical species that is found in the north-east area of the country.

- **The smallest frog** in the Southern Hemisphere is the gold frog. Adult gold frogs grow to just 9.8 mm in length.

- **The Galapagos tortoise** grows to 1.2 m in length. Their size and shell shapes vary according to which of the individual Galapagos Islands they originate from.

- **The reticulated python** is the world's longest snake. It can grow up to 10 m long and preys mainly on birds and mammals.

▲ *The giant treefrog of Australia is one of the biggest treefrogs in the world.*

> ···FASCINATING FACT···
> The smallest frog in the Northern
> Hemisphere has recently been discovered,
> and named *Eleutherodactylus iberia*.

Senses

▲ *Iguanas slowly stalk their prey, relying heavily on their sight to hunt.*

● **Wormlike amphibians** called caecilians spend their whole lives underground, so they do not have any use for eyes.

● **Frogs, toads and snakes** have something called a Jacobson's organ in the roof of their mouth. This helps them to 'taste' and 'smell' the outside world.

● **Snakes** have poor hearing and eyesight but they find prey by picking up vibrations travelling through the ground.

● **Frogs and toads** have large, well-developed eardrums and very good hearing.

● **Pit vipers**, such as rattlesnakes, can detect heat given off by prey through pits in their faces. They can even seek out prey in complete darkness.

● **Geckos and iguanas** have large eyes and very good eyesight. They are a type of lizard that cannot blink. Instead of having movable eyelids, like humans, they have fixed transparent 'spectacles' over their eyes.

● **One African gecko** has such thin skin over its ear-openings that if you were to look at it with the openings lined up precisely, you would see light coming through from the other end.

- **Some snakes** are entirely blind and live underground. They only emerge when lack of food forces them to the surface.

- **The olm** is a pale, thin, almost blind, cave-dwelling salamander from the lands bordering the Adriatic Sea.

▼ *The web-footed gecko from southwest Africa licks its eyes to keep them clean.*

> ...FASCINATING FACT...
> The African clawed toad has sense organs along its sides that detect vibrations from predators and prey.

9

Adaptable animals

- **Crocodiles** have a special flap in their throats that means that they can open their mouths underwater without breathing in water.

- **Chameleons have adapted** well to their life in trees. They have long toes that can grip branches firmly, and a long tail that holds onto other branches like another hand.

- **The flattened tails** of newts make them expert swimmers. They swim rather like fish, making an 's' shape as they move.

- **An amphibian's gills** enable it to breathe underwater. Blood flows inside the feathery gills at the same time as water flows over the outside. As the water flows past the gills, oxygen passes out of the water, straight into the blood of the amphibian.

- **The mudpuppy salamander's gills** change according to the oxygen content of its surroundings. In warmer water they tend to be larger, whilst in cooler water the gills shrink.

- **Most crocodiles** have eyes and nostrils at the top of their heads, which enable them to drift along just under the surface of the water unnoticed.

- **Caecilians** have a tentacle situated below each eye that enables them to locate prey by picking up on chemical signals.

- **As frogs swallow** their food, they tend to shut their eyes. This adds to the downward pressure and so assists the swallowing motion.

- **Some frogs** are adapted to living in trees. Their limbs are long and slim for gripping the branches, and their feet are specially adapted to enable them to climb vertically.

- **The rattlesnake** shakes the end of its tail as a warning and defence against predators.

▲ *The red-eyed treefrog has particularly long digits that enable it to cling onto branches.*

Dangerous enemies

- **The rat snake** catches and kills its prey by looping its body around the victim and crushing it to death.

- **The alligator snapping turtle** hunts with an open mouth. The turtle tempts fish with bait, and when the fish come to investigate, the turtle snaps its mouth shut and eats them up.

- **Poisonous snakes** inject venom into their prey. They do this through their grooved or hollow fangs.

- **The gila monster** from the desert areas of North America is one of only two venomous lizards in the world.

- **The gila monster's favourite food** is birds' eggs. It bites humans only in self-defence. Its brittle teeth may remain in the wound.

- **Bright patterns** on some amphibians' skin helps to deter predators. Their skin may be foul-tasting or cause irritation.

◀ *The gila monster from North America has strong limbs, making it an expert burrower.*

- **The poison fluid** from the skin of the poison-arrow frog is an effective pain killer in humans.

- **Without treatment**, victims of the taipan, black mamba, tiger snake, common krait and king cobra have a 50 to 100 percent risk of dying.

- **Sea snakes** in the Timor Sea have venom 100 times stronger than the taipan's.

- **The king cobra** is the longest venomous snake. It can grow to more than 4.5 m long.

▲ *The golden arrow-poison frog from Central and South America has skin glands that release venom. This is deadly to its predators but has been used to treat human heart attack victims.*

In the water

▲ *The king cobra is a good swimmer and spends much of its time around water. It is the longest venomous snake and when it is threatened it expands the hood around its head.*

- **Toads and frogs** swim by kicking with their hind legs. Their large, webbed feet act like flippers, helping them to push through water.

- **Sea snakes** can stay submerged for five hours and move rapidly through the depths.

- **European grass snakes** eat animals that live around the water, and so are expert swimmers.

- **The yellow-bellied sea snake** has a paddle-like end to its tail, to help it move swiftly through the water.

- **Floating sea snakes** often find themselves surrounded by fish who gather at their tail to avoid being eaten. When the snake fanices a snack it swims backwards, fooling the fish into thinking its head is its tail.

- **Sea turtles** have light, flat shells so they can move easily underwater.

- **Some sea turtles** have managed speeds of 29 km/h. Their flipper-like front legs 'fly' through the water. Their back legs form mini rudders for steering.

- **Water dragons** are mostly large tropical lizards that swim well by lashing their tails from side to side.

- **Terrapins** have wide feet with webbed toes, making them expert swimmers.

- **Many swimming snakes** have bands of colour along their bodies. This helps to break up their outline and blends them in with the ripples of the water.

Frog draws its legs up

Pushes its feet to the side

Begins to push legs back

The main kick propels the frog fowards

Frog begins to bring feet forwards

Frog's legs are pulled up, ready to go again

▲ *Frogs propel themselves forwards with their powerful back legs. Their webbed feet help them to push through the water more efficiently.*

Defence tactics

- **The European grass snake** pretends to be dead so that predators leave it alone. It rolls over onto its back, wiggles as if it is dying, and then lies still with its mouth open and its tongue hanging out.

- **The fire-bellied toad** has a bright red stomach. When it is threatened it leaps away to safety, and the quick flash of bright red confuses the attacker, giving the frog extra time to escape.

- **The female marsupial frog** carries her fertilized eggs in a pouch on her back to keep them safe.

- **The five-lined tree skunk lizard** has a detachable tail that enables it to escape when it is caught.

- **The chuckwalla lizard** jams itself into a rock crevice, then puffs its body up so that predators cannot pull it out.

- **The young blue-tongued** skink uses its bright blue tongue to startle predators.

- **The flying frog** of Southeast Asia is able to spread its webbed feet and glide from tree to tree. This helps it to escape predators by avoiding the ground.

◀ *The young blue-tongued skink has a bright blue mouth lining, and stripes along its body.*

● **The Australian shingleback lizard's tail** is shaped like its head. This confuses prey and so gives it a chance to escape.

● **When crocodiles** are threatened they can move quickly, almost appearing to leap out of the water. This is called tail-walking.

● **Iguanas' eyes** can swivel independently of each other, enabling them to keep a look out for prey and predators in all directions.

◀ *Iguanas blend in with their surroundings, so that they are hidden from predators and prey.*

17

Turtles and tortoises

- **Turtles and tortoises** are reptiles that live inside hard, armoured shells. Together with terrapins, they make up a group called the chelonians.

- **Turtles** live in the sea, freshwater, or on land. Tortoises live on land while terrapins live in streams and lakes.

- **The shield** on the back of a chelonian is called a carapace. Its flat belly armour is called a plastron.

- **Most turtles and tortoises** eat plants and tiny animals. They have no teeth, just jaws with very sharp edges.

▲ *Tortoises are very slow-moving and placid.*

- **Tortoises** live mostly in hot, dry regions and will hibernate in winter if brought to a cold country.

- **Turtles and tortoises** live to a great age. One giant tortoise found in 1766 in Mauritius lived 152 years.

- **The giant tortoise** grows to as long as 1.5 m.

- **The leatherback turtle** grows to as long as 2.5 m and weighs more than 800 kg.

- **Every three years,** green turtles gather together to swim thousands of kilometres to Ascension Island in the mid-Atlantic, where they lay their eggs ashore by moonlight at the highest tide. They bury the eggs in the sand, to be incubated by the heat of the Sun.

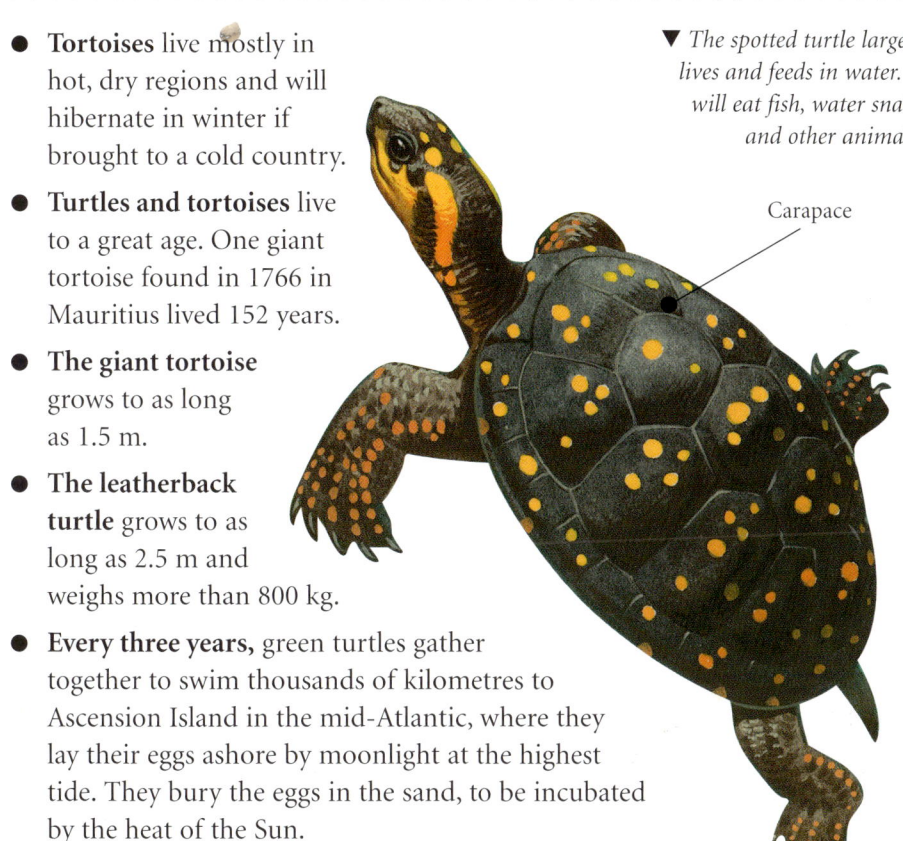

▼ *The spotted turtle largely lives and feeds in water. It will eat fish, water snails and other animals.*

Carapace

FASCINATING FACT
Giant tortoises were once kept on ships to provide fresh meat on long voyages.

Lizards

- **Lizards** are a group of 3800 scaly-skinned reptiles, varying from a few centimetres long to the 3 m-long Komodo dragon.

- **Lizards cannot** control their own body heat, and so rely on sunshine for warmth. This is why they live in warm climates and bask in the sun for hours each day.

- **Lizards move** in many ways – running, scampering and slithering. Some can glide. Unlike mammals, their limbs stick out sideways rather than downwards.

- **Most lizards** lay eggs, although a few give birth to live young. But unlike birds or mammals, a mother lizard does not nurture (look after) her young.

- **Most lizards** are meateaters, feeding on insects and other small creatures.

▲ Lizards have four legs and a long tail. In most lizards, the back legs are much stronger than the front, and are used to drive the animal forwards in a kind of writhing motion.

▶ *Geckos are small lizards that are mainly active at night. Their toes are are covered in hairy pads, which help them to stick to rough surfaces. Some geckos can even walk upside down.*

- **The glass lizard** has no legs. Its tail may break off and lie wriggling as a decoy if it is attacked. The lizard later grows another one.

- **The Australian frilled lizard** has a ruff around its neck. To put off attackers, it can spread out its ruff to make itself look three or four times bigger.

- **Horned lizards** can squirt a jet of blood from their eyes almost as far as 1 m to put off attackers.

- **The Komodo dragon** of Sumatra is the biggest lizard, weighing up to 150 kg or more. It can catch deer and pigs and swallow them whole.

> ...**FASCINATING FACT**...
> The Basilisk lizard is also known as the Jesus
> Christ lizard because it can walk on water.

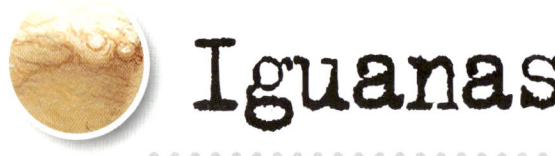

Iguanas

- **Iguanas** are large lizards that live around the Pacific and in the Americas.

- **Larger iguanas** are the only vegetarian lizards. Unlike other lizards, most eat fruit, flowers and leaves, rather than insects.

- **The common iguana** lives high up in trees, but lays its eggs in a hole in the ground.

▼ *Before each dive into water, marine iguanas warm themselves in the sunshine to gain energy.*

- **Common iguanas** will jump 6 m or more out of the trees to the ground if they are disturbed.

- **The rhinoceros iguana** of the West Indies gets its name from the pointed scales on its snout.

- **The marine iguana** of the Galapagos Islands is the only lizard that spends much of its life in the sea.

- **Marine iguanas** keep their eggs warm ready for hatching in the mouth of volcanoes, risking death to put them there.

- **When in the water,** a marine iguana may dive for 15 minutes or more, pushing itself along with its tail.

- **Although marine iguanas** cannot breathe underwater, their heart rate slows so that they use less oxygen.

- **The chuckwalla** inflates its body with air to wedge itself in a rock crack if it is in danger.

▶ *There are 700 plus species of iguana, nearly all of which live in the Americas. Like most lizards, iguanas hatch from eggs.*

Chameleons

- **Chameleons** are 85 species of lizard, most of which live on the island of Madagascar and in mainland Africa.

- **The smallest chameleon**, the dwarf Brookesia, could balance on your little finger. The biggest, Oustalet's chameleon, is the size of a small cat.

- **A chameleon** can look forwards and backwards at the same time, as each of its amazing eyes can swivel in all directions independently of the other.

- **Chameleons feed** on insects and spiders, hunting them in trees by day.

- **A chameleon's tongue** is almost as long as its body, but is normally squashed up inside its mouth.

▼ *The chameleon can shoot out its tongue to a great length.*

▶ *Most of a chameleon's bulging eyes are protected by skin.*

● **A chameleon shoots** out its tongue in a fraction of a second to trap its victim on a sticky pad at the tip.

● **The chameleon's tongue** is fired out from a special launching bone on its lower jaw.

● **Most lizards** can change colour, but chameleons are experts, changing quickly to all sorts of colours.

● **Chameleons change colour** when they are angry or frightened, too cold or too hot, or sick – but they change colour less often to match their surroundings.

● **The colour** of the skin is controlled by pigment cells called melanophores, which change colour as they change size.

25

Pythons and boas

- **Constrictors** are snakes that squeeze their victims to death, rather than poisoning them. They include pythons, boas and anacondas.

- **A constrictor** does not crush its victim. Instead, it winds itself around, gradually tightening its coils until the victim suffocates.

- **Constrictors usually swallow** victims whole, then spend days digesting them. They have special jaws that allow their mouths to open very wide. A large meal can be seen as a lump moving down the body.

▼ *Pythons are tropical snakes that live in moist forests in Asia and Africa. They are the world's biggest snakes, rivalled only by giant anacondas. Pythons are one long tube of muscle, well able to squeeze even big victims to death. They usually eat animals about the size of domestic cats, but occasionally they go for really big meals such as wild pigs and deer.*

- **Pythons** are big snakes that live in Asia, Indonesia and Africa. In captivity, reticulated pythons grow to 9 m. Boas and anacondas are the big constrictors of South America.

- **Boas** capture their prey by lying in wait, hiding motionless under trees and waiting for victims to pass by. Like all snakes, they can go for many weeks without eating.

- **Like many snakes**, most constrictors begin life as eggs. Unusually for snakes, female pythons look after their eggs until they hatch by coiling around them. Even more unusually, Indian and green tree pythons actually keep their eggs warm by shivering.

- **Female boas** do not lay eggs, giving birth to live young.

- **Boas** have tiny remnants of back legs, called spurs, which males use to tickle females during mating.

- **Anacondas** spend much of their lives in swampy ground or shallow water, lying in wait for victims to come and drink. One anaconda was seen to swallow a 2 m-long caiman (a kind of crocodile).

- **When frightened,** the royal python of Africa coils itself into a tight ball, which is why it is sometimes called the ball python. Rubber boas do the same, but hide their heads and stick their tails out aggressively to fool attackers.

> ...FASCINATING FACT...
> A 4 to 5 m-long African rock python was once seen to swallow an entire 60 kg impala (a kind of antelope) whole – horns and all.

Cobras and vipers

● **Two kinds of poisonous snake** are dangerous to humans – vipers and elapids such as cobras and mambas.

● **Elapids** have their venom (poison) in short front fangs. A viper's fangs are so long that they usually have to be folded away.

● **The hamadryad cobra** of Southeast Asia is the world's largest poisonous snake, growing to over 5 m.

● **In India,** cobras kill more than 7000 people every year. The bite of a king cobra can kill an elephant in 4 hours. The marine cobra lives in the sea and its venom is 100 times more deadly.

● **Snake charmers** use the spectacled cobra, playing to it so that it follows the pipe as if about to strike – but the snake's fangs have been removed to make it safe.

▶ *When on the defensive, a cobra rears up and spreads the skin of its neck in a hood to make it look bigger. This often gives victims a chance to hit it away.*

● **A spitting cobra** squirts venom into its attacker's eyes, and is accurate at 2 m or more. The venom is not deadly, but it blinds the victim and is very painful.

- **The black mamba** of Africa can race along at 25 km/h with its head raised and its tongue flickering.

- **A viper's venom** kills its victims by making their blood clot. Viper venom has been used to treat haemophiliacs (people whose blood does not clot well).

- **The pit vipers** of the Americas hunt their warm-blooded victims using heat-sensitive pits on the side of their heads.

▶ *The wedge-shaped head, narrow neck and brown-green scale pattern of the Gaboon viper make this snake almost impossible to spot among the leaves of the forest floor. It has the longest fangs of any viper, up to 5 cm.*

...FASCINATING FACT...
Fer-de-lance snakes have 60 to 80 babies, each of which is deadly poisonous.

29

Crocodiles and alligators

- **Crocodiles, alligators, caimans and gharials** are large reptiles that together form the group known as crocodilians. There are 14 species of crocodile, 7 alligators and caimans, and 1 gharial.

- **Crocodilian species** lived alongside the dinosaurs 200 million years ago, and they are the nearest we have to living dinosaurs today.

- **Crocodilians are hunters** that lie in wait for animals coming to drink at the water's edge. When crocodilians seize a victim they drag it into the water, stun it with a blow from their tail, then drown it.

- **Like all reptiles,** crocodilians get their energy from the Sun. Typically, they bask in the sunshine on a sandbar or the river bank in the morning, then slip into the river at midday to cool off.

▶ *Crocodiles are huge reptiles with powerful bodies, scaly skin and great snapping jaws.*

The crocodile's eyes and nostrils are raised so it can see and breathe while floating underwater

A crocodile will often kill its victims with a swipe from its strong tail

The skin on the back has ridges formed by dozens of tiny bones called osteoderms

- **Crocodiles live** in tropical rivers and swamps. At over 5 m long, saltwater crocodiles are the world's largest reptiles – one grew to over 8 m long.

- **Crocodiles** are often said to cry after eating their victims. In fact only saltwater crocodiles cry, and they do it to get rid of salt, not because they are sorry.

- **Crocodiles have thinner snouts** than alligators, and a fourth tooth on the lower jaw that is visible when the crocodile's mouth is shut.

- **The female Nile crocodile** lays her eggs in nests that she digs in sandy river banks, afterwards covering the eggs in sand to keep them at a steady temperature. When the babies hatch they make loud piping calls. The mother then digs them out and carries them one by one in her mouth to the river.

- **Alligators** are found both in the Florida Everglades in the United States and in the Yangtze River in China.

The skin on the belly is smooth and was once prized as a material for shoes and handbags

> ...**FASCINATING FACT**...
> Crocodilians often swallow stones to help
> them stay underwater for long periods.
> Without this ballast, they might tip over.

Amphibian fact file

▲ *The strawberry poison-dart frog from Central America relies on poison to keep enemies at bay.*

- **Amphibians** are common in cooler, damper parts of the world. They like wet places and spend part of their life in water and part on land.

- **When the weather** turns especially cold, amphibians often hibernate. They burrow into mud at the bottom of ponds or under stones and logs.

- **As spring arrives** amphibians come out of hiding. The warmer weather sees many of them returning to the pond or stream where they were born.

- **Amphibians sometimes** have long journeys back to their birthplace, and often they have to travel through towns and over busy roads.

- **In some countries**, signs warn drivers of the unusual hazard of frogs or toads crossing the road to return to breeding grounds.

- **Journeys to breeding grounds** may be up to 5 km long, which is a long way for an animal that measures just a few centimetres in length.

- **Some amphibians** are able to breathe through their thin skin. Oxygen from the air passes directly into their blood stream.

- **Amphibians** have poison glands in their skin. These produce secretions that are toxic and so help to protect them from predators.

- **Some salamanders** are lungless. They absorb oxygen through their skin and the lining of their mouth. This means the skin must always stay moist. If it dries, oxygen cannot pass through.

- **Most amphibians** rely on their sight to hunt, and tend to have large eyes because they are active at night.

▶ *This aquatic salamander is called a mudpuppy. It lives in freshwater lakes, rivers and streams in North America.*

Frogs and toads

- **Frogs** and toads are amphibians – creatures that live both on land and in the water.

- **There are about 3500 species** of frog and toad. Most live near water, but some live in trees and others live underground.

- **Frogs** are mostly smaller and better jumpers. Toads are bigger, with thicker, wartier skin that holds on to moisture and allows them to live on land longer.

◄ *Frogs are superb jumpers, with long back legs to propel them into the air. Most also have suckers on their fingers to help them land securely on slippery surfaces.*

- **Frogs and toads** are meateaters. They catch fast-moving insects by darting out their long, sticky tongues.

- **Frogs and toads begin life** as fishlike tadpoles, hatching in the water from huge clutches of eggs called spawn.

- **After 7 to 10 weeks**, tadpoles grow legs and lungs and develop into frogs ready to leave the water.

- **In midwife toads**, the male looks after the eggs, not the female – winding strings of eggs around his back legs and carrying them about until they hatch.

- **The male Darwin's frog** swallows the eggs and keeps them in his throat until they hatch – and pop out of his mouth.

- **The Goliath frog** of West Africa is the largest frog – at over 25 cm long. The biggest toad is the cane toad of Queensland, Australia – one weighed 2.6 kg and measured 50 cm in length with its legs outstretched. The cane toad was introduced to Australia from South America to help control pests.

- **The arrow-poison frogs** that live in the tropical rainforests of Central America get their name because natives tip their arrows with deadly poison from glands in the frogs' skin. Many arrow-poison frogs are very colourful.

▶ *The natterjack toad is easily recognized by a distinctive yellow line down its head and back. It gives off a smell of burning rubber when alarmed.*

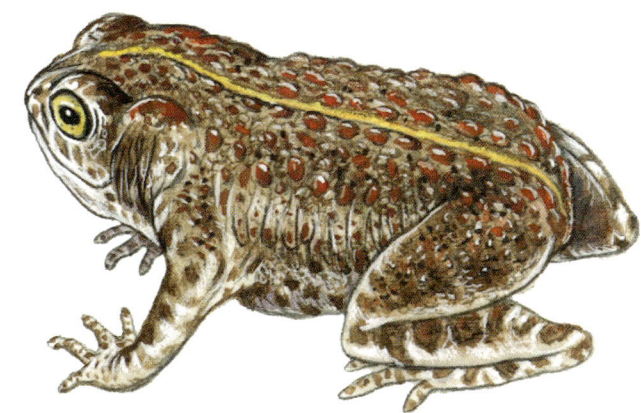

Newts and salamanders

- **Newts and salamanders** are carnivorous and eat insects, snails and worms.

- **The name 'newt'** is given to the type of amphibian that spends the majority of its life in water.

- **Newts are largely inactive** creatures, and so do not feed frequently. If food is readily available, they tend to store fat, so that in colder months they can survive for longer without feeding.

- **As they have** small heads and eyes they rely heavily upon their sense of smell to hunt.

- **Newts and salamanders** tend to be well camouflaged, with skin patterns and colours that enable them to hide. However, some species are brightly coloured, often to indicate to predators that they are toxic (poisonous).

- **Some species do not** produce toxic substances, but are still brightly coloured. This is a highly effective defence against predators.

- **Several species** are able to detach their tale. When they are attacked the twitching tale distracts the predator, giving the newt or salamander a greater chance of escape.

- **The male great crested newt** becomes more colourful to attract a mate. He develops a bright red underside and a frilly back crest.

- **If the Chinese spiny newt** is seized by a predator it pushes its sharp-tipped ribs through its skin. The ribs pass through its skin glands on the way and release an extremely unpleasant poison.

- **In most salamander species** the male leaves a 'packet' of sperm on the ground, which the female then takes into her body.

36

▲ *The yellow-eyed salamander lives on the forest floor. It has large eyes because it is nocturnal. It relies heavily on its sense of smell to find food.*

...FASCINATING FACT...
The fire salamander is so called because it often hibernates in logs, which may then be collected and used as firewood.

37

Amphibian life cycle

- **Most amphibians** are born and grow up in fresh water such as ponds, pools, streams and rivers.

- **Amphibians move** onto dry land when they are adults and return to water to breed.

- **As they grow**, amphibians completely change their appearance. This change is called metamorphosis.

- **The young** of amphibians are called larvae. For example, tadpoles are the larvae of frogs and toads, and most newts and salamanders.

- **Amphibian larvae** can survive in water because they can breathe through large, feathery flaps called gills that can take oxygen from the water.

- **Some salamanders** lay their eggs in damp places, such as under stones or logs, or in moss. Others attach them to rocks underwater. The number of eggs laid varies between four or five to more than 5000.

- **The axolotl** is a North American salamander that has never developed beyond the larval stage. It develops just enough to breed.

- **The male** South American Surinam toad mates underwater and presses the eggs onto his mate's back. The eggs remain there until they hatch.

- **Most amphibians** lay soft eggs. These may be in a jelly-like string, or clump of tiny eggs called spawn, as with frogs and toads. Newts lay their eggs singly.

- **The fire salamander** gives birth to live young. The eggs stay inside the mother, where the young hatch out and develop. She then gives birth to young that are much like miniature adults.

A froglet loses its tail and
grows into an adult frog

Adult toad

Frog spawn (eggs) float
on top of fresh water

Tadpoles hatch
from the eggs

Adult newt

Tadpoles grow legs
and change into
froglets

Index